Bob Chilcott

T0088395

Times and Seasons

8 SONGS FOR UPPER VOICES

MUSIC DEPARTMENT

OXFORD
UNIVERSITY PRESS

OXFORD
UNIVERSITY PRESS

Great Clarendon Street, Oxford OX2 6DP,
United Kingdom

Oxford University Press is a department of the University of Oxford.
It furthers the University's objective of excellence in research, scholarship,
and education by publishing worldwide. Oxford is a registered trade mark of
Oxford University Press in the UK and in certain other countries

© Oxford University Press 2019

Bob Chilcott has asserted his right under the Copyright, Designs
and Patents Act, 1988, to be identified as the Composer of these Works

Database right Oxford University Press (maker)

First published 2019

Impression: 1

All rights reserved. No part of this publication may be reproduced,
stored in a retrieval system, or transmitted, in any form or by any means,
without the prior permission in writing of Oxford University Press

Permission to perform the works in this anthology in public
(except in the course of divine worship) should normally be obtained
from the Performing Right Society Ltd (PRS) at www.prsformusic.com
or a local performing right licensing organization, unless the owner or the
occupier of the premises being used already holds a licence from such an
organization. Likewise, permission to make and exploit a recording must
be obtained in advance from the Mechanical-Copyright Protection
Society Ltd (MCPS) at www.prsformusic.com or a local mechanical
copyright licensing organization

Enquiries concerning reproduction outside the scope of the above should be
directed to the Music Rights Department, Oxford University Press, at
music.permissions.uk@oup.com or at the address above

ISBN 978-0-19-353088-1

Music and text origination by
Katie Johnston
Printed in Great Britain on acid-free paper by
Halstan & Co. Ltd, Amersham, Bucks.

Contents

Morning	4
Spring	6
Midday	12
Summer	14
Evening	20
Autumn	23
Night	28
Winter	32

Composer's note

This collection of songs casts the times of the day and the seasons of the year in a voice of youthful optimism. The new poems have been specially written by Delphine Chalmers, who at the time of writing is about to begin her third year as an undergraduate at the University of Oxford. Delphine's tender and elegant words suggested pairing *a cappella* folk-like melodies for the times of day with more rhapsodic, accompanied songs for the seasons of the year. The pairs of songs (a time and a season each) were written for three school choirs, from Japan, Australia, and England (Delphine's old school), and a renowned children's choir from Germany, with whom I have worked over the last few years. These pieces can be sung together as a set or separately as stand-alone songs.

for Keisuke Nakajima and the Kurume Shin-ai High School Choir, Fukuoka, Japan

Morning

Delphine Chalmers
(b. 1998)

BOB CHILCOTT
(b. 1955)

Duration: 2 mins

Music © Oxford University Press 2019. Text © Delphine Chalmers 2019. Photocopying this copyright material is ILLEGAL.

21
mf
yes - ter - day And make each foot - step glit - ter, and
24
make each foot - step glit - ter, glit - ter.
unis.
28
p dolce
Like a flower that strives to grow I long to crane my neck.
31
Find - ing in your warmth the life, the life that will fuse me
34
mp
to this world And hold my quest - ing roots firm, and
37
hold my quest - ing roots firm, my quest - ing roots
40
mf
firm And know I am re - born, and
43
rit.
mp
p
know I am re - born, I am re - born.

for Keisuke Nakajima and the Kurume Shin-ai High School Choir, Fukuoka, Japan

Spring

Delphine Chalmers
(b. 1998)

BOB CHILCOTT
(b. 1955)

Duration: 3 mins

Music © Oxford University Press 2019. Text © Delphine Chalmers 2019. Photocopying this copyright material is ILLEGAL.

10
dew - y cob - webs cast their nets
To catch soft bird - song in their
12
mp
S.
A.
unis.
sil - ver threads.
So, I'll un - furl
my hands,
Let my
mp
14
unis.
chry - sa - lis heart speak.
I'll un - furl
my thoughts
And
16
p
set my winged i - ma - gin - a - tion
free.
p

19
S.
A.
mp
ah
ah
mp più espress.
To-day is one of those days When the sky roars by in a co-balt blaze,
mp più espress.
22
ah
Dom-ing far a - bove our reach. To-day is one of those days
25
ah
ah
When the trees stretch out their fin - gers

27
mf
ah
So, I'll un -
mf
To grasp de - light with rust - ling palms.
So, I'll un -
mf
29
S.
A.
unis.
-furl my hands, Let my chry-sa - lis heart speak. I'll un -
31
unis.
-furl my thoughts And set my winged i - ma - gin - a - tion
33
mp
free.
p dolce
To-day is one of those days
mp
p dolce

36
When I see the beau-ty of the world Gleam-ing out - ward
39
from with-in. To-day is one of those days And I
42
know that I am blessed To see the spi - rit that drives each
44
mp
unis.
liv - ing thing. So, I'll un - furl my hands, Let my
mp

46
unis.
chry - sa - lis heart speak. I'll un - furl my thoughts And
48
mf
unis.
set my winged i - ma-gin - a - tion free. So I'll un - furl my hands, Let my
mf
51
unis.
chry-sa - lis heart speak. I'll un - furl my thoughts And
53
rit.
mp
pp
set my winged i-ma - gin-a - tion free.
mp
pp

for Jenny Moon and Bel Canto, Hillcrest Christian College, Queensland, Australia

Midday

Delphine Chalmers
(b. 1998)

BOB CHILCOTT
(b. 1955)

Lightly ♩ = *c.*69

unis. ***mp***

SOPRANO
ALTO

Mid - day is a qui - et gard'n - er:

3

She holds the hour in her palm. If you

mf

S.

A.

5

steal up - on her gent - ly She will let you see How her

più legato

7

poco rit.

unis. ***mp***

fin - gers sow the se - conds With poised se - re - ni - ty.

9

a tempo

Our morn - ing blooms de - light her:

11

She ga - thers them in her arms And

mf

Duration: 1.5 mins

Music © Oxford University Press 2019. Text © Delphine Chalmers 2019. Photocopying this copyright material is ILLEGAL.

13
più legato
if you ask her kind - ly She will let you see The
poco rit.
15
unis. mp
snow-drop grins and li - ly tears, The for - get - me-nots of his - to -
a tempo
17
mf
- ry. And when the fi - nal se - cond lands
20
f
She will stretch out her palms And
22
più legato
if you love her wise - ly She will let you take The
rit.
24
unis.
mp
p
fu - ture from her fin - gers: Your gar - den is your own to make.

for Jenny Moon and Bel Canto, Hillcrest Christian College, Queensland, Australia

Summer

Delphine Chalmers
(b. 1998)

BOB CHILCOTT
(b. 1955)

Duration: 2 mins

Music © Oxford University Press 2019. Text © Delphine Chalmers 2019. Photocopying this copyright material is ILLEGAL.

7
light finds the motes of me-mo-ry The years have hid-den from view And
9
S. f
A.
makes me, and makes me dream a-gain. In
12
sum-mer, sum - mer,
f
14
mf più dolce
unis.
sum-mer, sum - mer. You
mf più dolce

17
shared my worlds and dap-pled dens, my worlds and dap - pled dens, The
19
first stings that taught me how to feel. With
21
fruit - bruised lips and sun - brown legs I chased with length'n - ing strides The
23
f
sha - dow of who I might be-come. In

26
sum - mer,
sum - mer,
f
28
sum-mer,
mf più dolce
sum - mer.
mf più dolce
31
unis.
Though you end in au - burn splen - dour, In
33
mists that cloud milk - y skies, You are

35
mp
al - ways there for me in whis - pers, in
37
S.
whis - pers, whis - pers.
f
ah
A.
whis - pers, whis - pers.
f
ah ah
mp
f
40
ah ah
ah
ah

43
ah
In sum - mer,
ah
Sum-mer,
46
mf più dolce
mp
sum - mer,
in sum-mer,
mf più dolce
mp
sum-mer,
in sum-mer,
mf più dolce
mp
49
rit.
p
in sum - mer,
in sum-mer.
p
in sum - mer,
in sum-mer.
rit.
p

for Stephen Willis and the choir of The Abbey School, Reading

Evening

Delphine Chalmers
(b. 1998)

BOB CHILCOTT
(b. 1955)

Flowing ♩. = *c.*56

SOPRANO

p dolce

Eve - ning comes in vel - vet sha - dows, In ease - ful soft - ness

ALTO

p dolce

oo *oo*

5

and in rest. Her sky is stitched with sil - ver threads, With

oo

9

poco cresc. *mp*

cos - mic pat-terns and with runes. Her black bats flut - ter

poco cresc. *mp*

oo Her black bats flut - ter

13

rit. *p*

like my heart, My ma - gic cloak of imp - ish tricks, imp - ish tricks.

p

like my heart, My ma - gic cloak of imp - ish tricks, imp - ish tricks.

Duration: 2 mins

Music © Oxford University Press 2019. Text © Delphine Chalmers 2019. Photocopying this copyright material is ILLEGAL.

a tempo
18
p dolce
Let me lose my - self in star - light, In me - mo - ries and
p dolce
oo
oo
22
hushed words. Let me dance in street lamp sput - ters, Be -
oo
26
poco cresc.
mp
- neath cas - cad - ing gut - ters Un - til my wor - ries
poco cresc.
mp
oo
Un - til my wor - ries
rit.
30
p
fade a - way And I am in - can - de - scent, in - can - de - scent.
p
fade a - way And I am in - can - de - scent, in - can - de - scent.

a tempo
35
p dolce
Eve - ning comes in vel - vet sha - dows, In ease - ful soft - ness
p dolce
oo
oo
39
and in rest. Her lungs are filled with gen - tle sounds, With
oo
43
poco cresc.
mp
hoots and whis - pered mus - ings, Spell - soft sounds and
poco cresc.
mp
oo
Spell - soft sounds and
47
rit.
p
in - can - ta - tions, My sym-phon-ic sor - cer - ess, sor - cer- ess.
p
in - can - ta - tions, My sym-phon-ic sor - cer - ess, sor - cer- ess.

for Stephen Willis and the choir of The Abbey School, Reading

Autumn

Delphine Chalmers
(b. 1998)

BOB CHILCOTT
(b. 1955)

Duration: 2 mins

Music © Oxford University Press 2019. Text © Delphine Chalmers 2019. Photocopying this copyright material is ILLEGAL.

7
mp
neck is draped in horse - chest - nut beads, Her
mp
9
cresc.
S.
A.
mf
mp
hands gleam with ru - by rings Just for you and me But
cresc.
mf
mp
11
unis.
f
what, what can we of - fer? The
f
14
stars of dew shi-ver on your tongue, Sil - ver mouth - fuls nour - ish - ing our

16
mf
world. Her mists are steam on a la - den spoon, Her
mf
18
mp
wealth is a stur - dy, stur - dy pump - kin gourd, Her
mp cresc.
20
cresc.
mf
mp
unis.
mes-sage is a self-less love Just for you and me But what, what can we
mf
mp
23
mf
of - fer?
p

25
mp
Sense! Sense the earth's beau - ty, Sense it through your dap - pled
mp
28
mf
fin - ger-tips, Through the or-chard glit - ter of your eyes,
mf
31
through the or - chard glit - ter of your eyes
33
f
And be filled with wind - fall joy, A fond - ness for each flick-er-ing, flick-er-ing
f

35
mf cresc.
thing.
To - ge - ther we can of - fer the
mf cresc.
37
f
unis. mf
har - vest of our hearts,
the har-vest of our
f
mf
39
rit.
mp
hearts,
the har-vest of our
mp
41
p
hearts,
the har-vest of our hearts.
p

for Hans de Gilde, Barbara Comes, and the Ulmer Spatzen Chor

Night

Delphine Chalmers
(b. 1998)

BOB CHILCOTT
(b. 1955)

Quiet but spirited ♩. = *c.*96

SOPRANO

p

Be-neath the glass - y o - ceans, the o - ceans of my eyes, The

ALTO

p

oo

3

pearl - y king of fa - thoms Is bear - ing jag - ged teeth And

mf

oo *oo* And

5

sud - den - ly he's div - ing And I'm cling - ing to his tail As he

sud - den - ly he's div - ing And I'm cling - ing to his tail As he

7

signs his ink - y tre - ble clef in waves.

signs his ink - y tre - ble clef in waves.

9

f

Trea-sure the lives you live in dreams And the dreams you live in life.

f

Trea-sure the lives you live in dreams And the dreams you live in life.

Duration: 2 mins

Music © Oxford University Press 2019. Text © Delphine Chalmers 2019. Photocopying this copyright material is ILLEGAL.

11
Make each snore a shib-bo - leth, Each mut - tered word a pro-mise To un -
Make each snore a shib-bo - leth, Each mut - tered word a pro-mise To un -
13
-lock the rich - es that are yours, To trust in the hope - ful heart
-lock the rich - es that are yours, To trust in the hope - ful heart
15
mf
You car - ry as you jour - ney on.
mf
You car - ry as you jour - ney on.
18
p
Deep in - side the black hole, the black hole of my pu - pils,
p
oo
20
mf
Ev - 'ry con - stel - la - tion, con - stel - la - tion col - lides And
mf
oo
oo
And

22
sud - den - ly I'm float - ing And the peace of e - ter - ni - ty holds me. I shall
sud - den - ly I'm float - ing And the peace of e - ter - ni - ty holds me. I shall
24
lose my - self in the mu - sic of the spheres.
lose my - self in the mu - sic of the spheres.
26
f
Trea-sure the lives you live in dreams And the dreams you live in life.
f
Trea-sure the lives you live in dreams And the dreams you live in life.
28
Make each snore a shib-bo - leth, Each mut - tered word a pro-mise To un -
Make each snore a shib-bo - leth, Each mut - tered word a pro-mise To un -
30
-lock the rich - es that are yours, To trust in the hope - ful heart
-lock the rich - es that are yours, To trust in the hope - ful heart

32
mf
You car - ry as you jour - ney on.
mf
You car - ry as you jour - ney on.
35
f
Trea-sure the lives you live in dreams And the dreams you live in life.
f
Trea-sure the lives you live in dreams And the dreams you live in life.
37
Make each snore a shib-bo - leth, Each mut - tered word a pro-mise To un -
Make each snore a shib-bo - leth, Each mut - tered word a pro-mise To un -
39
-lock the rich - es that are yours, To trust in the hope - ful heart
-lock the rich - es that are yours, To trust in the hope - ful heart
rit.
41
mp
p
You car - ry as you jour - ney on.
mp
p
You car - ry as you jour - ney on.

for Hans de Gilde, Barbara Comes, and the Ulmer Spatzen Chor

Winter

Delphine Chalmers
(b. 1998)

BOB CHILCOTT
(b. 1955)

Duration: 3 mins

Music © Oxford University Press 2019. Text © Delphine Chalmers 2019. Photocopying this copyright material is ILLEGAL.

10
We've got our skates on.
13
We can't see for snow - drifts
But what do we care?
16
What do we care?
unis.
We've got our
19
skates on.
mf sost.

22
mf
So, we'll tip and tum-ble o - ver ice, tum-ble o - ver ice, we'll
25
tip and tum-ble o - ver ice, tum-ble o - ver ice. Our coats will glis-ten in for-
28
-bid-den moon-light, our coats will glis-ten in for - bid-den moon-light As our
31
f
feet etch out our names, our names to - night.
f

35
We can't see for snow - drifts
But what do we care?
38
What do we care?
We've got our
41
skates on.
We can't see for snow-
44
- drifts
But what do we care?

47
unis.
What do we care?
We've got our skates on.
mf sost.
50
mf
So, we'll
53
leave our foot-prints in the snow, foot-prints in the snow, we'll leave our foot-prints in the snow,
56
foot-prints in the snow. Our joy-ful words will hang in the crys - tal air, our

59
joy - ful words will hang in the crys - tal air As we re - vel in the
62
f
breath - less youth we share. We can't see for snow-
f
66
- drifts But what do we care?
69
What do we care? We've got our skates on.

72
We can't see for snow - drifts
75
But what do we care?
What do we care?
78
unis.
We've got our skates on.
mp
82
mp
So, we'll snug-gle up be-fore the hearth, be-fore the hearth, we'll

85
snug-gle up be-fore the hearth, be-fore the hearth. With flames that spar - kle
88
mf
in our eyes, with flames that spar - kle in our eyes, As we
mf
91
f
wrap our friend-ship up in rib - bon ties.
f
95
We can't see for snow - drifts But what do we care?

98
What do we care?
We've got our
101
skates on.
We can't see for snow-
104
- drifts
But what do we care?
107
What do we care?
unis. ff
We've got our skates on.
ff